MEXICO

WHITE STAR
PUBLISHERS

Text by
Pietro Tarallo

Graphic design
Anna Galliani

Map
Cristina Franco

Translation by
Barbara Fisher

Contents

1 *San Cristóbal de Las Casas, Chiapas. Set on the hill that rises to the north-east of the old centre, the façade of the Church of Nostra Señora de Guadalupe is brilliant white with ochre-yellow pilaster strips and scrolls.*

2-3 *Uxmal, Yucatán. An ancient Mayan city, Uxmal is known mainly for its Pyramid of the Magician. Built to a semi-elliptical plan and 128 feet high, it stands in the centre of ruins scattered over 247 acres; a giddy flight of steps on the main façade leads to the top and the doorway, shaped like the gaping mouth of the god Chac.*

4-5 *Misol-Ha, Chiapas. The picture shows how this region is still extensively covered with lush, tropical vegetation.*

6-7 *Cancún, Quintana Roo. The Las Vegas of the Caribbean since the Seventies, Cancún has become one of the most famous holiday resorts in the world. The lagoon is surrounded by a white sandy beach filled with towering skyscrapers and luxury hotels in the most bizarre shapes and sizes.*

8 *Oaxaca. This delightful capital of the state of the same name still conserves splendid colonial monuments and age-old traditions that are repeated every year in the grandiose celebration of* Los Lunes del Cerro, *held on the first two Mondays after July 16.*

9 *Chichén Itzá, Yucatán. This major Mayan site dates from the late classic period and boasts many extremely interesting monuments: one is the spectacular Temple of the Thousand Columns with an altar representing the god Chac-mool on its platform.*

© 2003 White Star S.r.l.
Via C. Sassone, 22/24
13100 Vercelli, Italy
www.whitestar.it

ISBN 88-540-0028-0

REPRINTS:
1 2 3 4 5 6   07 06 05 04 03

Printed in Singapore by Star Standard Color separation by Magenta, Lit. Con, Singapore

The Publisher would like to thank the following for their valuable assistance in the making of this book: Air France, Mexican Tourist Board in Rome, SECTUR in Mexico City, the local tourist boards of the various Mexican states, Giuseppe Marcelletti of Marcelletti Tour, Hotel Stouffer Presidente and Hotel Nikko in Mexico City.

12-13 *Lake Pátzcuaro, Michoacán. Fishermen using the traditional butterfly nets are an increasingly rare sight on this lake. At the centre of this sheet of water is the little Isla Janitzio, famous for its local craftwork.*

14-15 *Tula, Hidalgo. The Toltec capital appeared around the 7th century A.D. and reached its peak of splendour between the 10th and 12th centuries. The picture shows the four huge, basalt telamones that adorn the summit of the Temple of Quetzalcóatl.*

Gulf of Mexico
CUBA
CANCÚN
MÉRIDA
CHICHÉN ITZÁ
CAMPECHE
YUCATÁN
TULUM
CARIBBEAN SEA
TABASCO LOWLAND
VILLAHERMOSA
ISTHUMUS OF TEHUANTEPEC
PALEQUE
BELIZE
SAN CRISTÓBAL DE LAS CASAS
CAÑON DEL SUMIDERO
OCOSINGO
MAR MUERTO
GUATEMALA

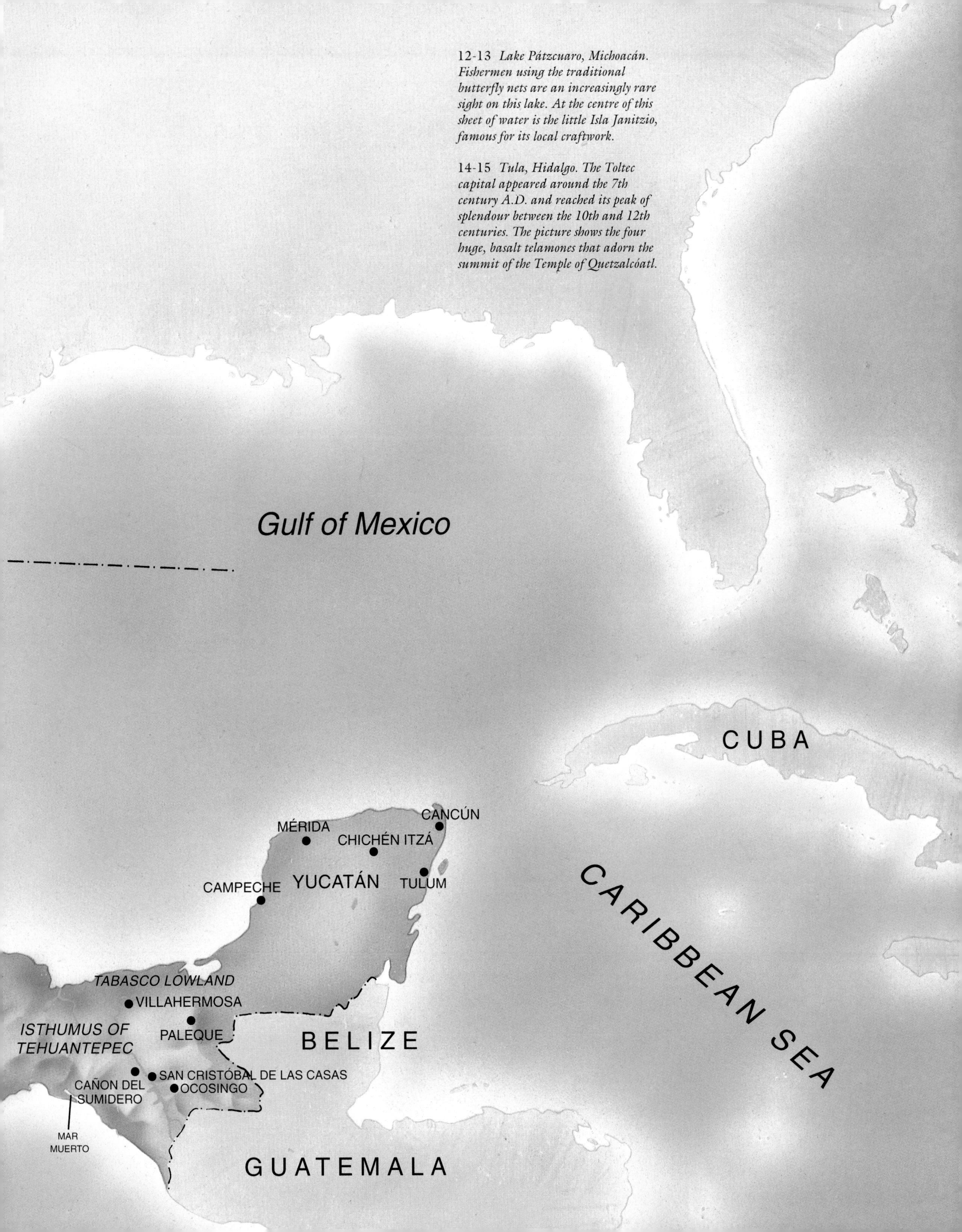

Introduction

"Unbroken, eternally resistant, it was a people that lived without hope, and without care. Gay even, and laughing with indifferent carelessness. ... These handsome natives! Was it because they were death-worshippers, Moloch-worshippers, that they were so uncowed and handsome? Their pure acknowledgement of death, and their undaunted admission of nothingness kept so erect and careless." Thus wrote D.H. Lawrence (1885-1930) in 1926 in his novel "The Plumed Serpent". Set in a fascinating and cruel Mexico this is one of the English writer's finest books; it reveals how much ancient symbolism has survived unchanged over the centuries and the lasting magic that binds these peoples to their past. But "The Plumed Serpent", the terrible god Quetzalcoatl, is also a symbol of huge importance in pre-Colombian civilizations, representing the union between heaven and earth.

Life and death, pleasure and pain, wealth and poverty, happiness and sorrow, laughter and tears, gaiety and gloom, prosperity and starvation, joy and grief, success and misfortune - in Mexico these are the opposite sides of the same coin. The heads and tails of a mysterious destiny willed by inscrutable ancient deities and more recent ones alike: the gods, cruel and bloodthirsty, of the Olympus of the Mesoamerican religions and the Trinity and Saints, solemn and compassionate, of the Catholic Heaven imposed with Cross and Sword.

This timeless tale, steeped in mystery and riddled with pain, that started many thousands of years ago, continues to the present day.

It all commenced 65 million years ago with a crescent of fire, mixed with lava and lapilli, flames and incandescent metals. The Mexican territory was formed during the Cainozoic era. That was the time of the huge eruptions that resulted in the emergence of the continental mass and the folding which, later, formed the lateral and southern mountain chains. Countless volcanic cones (more than 100) still tower above the highest peaks of the Sierra Madre Occidental, to the west, and the Sierra Madre Oriental, to the east, which close the Mexican Altiplano. The two longitudinal mountain chains, the natural extension of the

Rocky Mountains, gradually push south to join up south east of Puebla with the Sierra Madre del Sur range. This is the very heart of the country, where the Popocatépetl (about 17,820 feet) and the Iztaccíhuatl (a little more than 17,340 feet) volcanoes rise.

In the southern regions the Cordillera suddenly drops to the 700 feet of the Isthsmus of Tehuantepec. After this come the Chiapas mountain region, the swampy lowlands of Tabasco and the flat peninsula of Yucatán, geologically in Central America.

Mexico is like a huge "crescent moon" arched between North America and Central America, from the United States to Belize and Guatemala; a vast territory (761,600 square miles) enclosed between the Tropic of Cancer and the Caribbean Sea, the Pacific Ocean and the Gulf of Mexico; a spectacular country where over thousands of years, nature has created landscapes and scenery of unequalled beauty.

What is most striking is the incredibly varied, complex and multiform vegetation. There are 30,000 plant and flower species, among which are 1,000 orchids, and 22% of the total surface area is wood and forest.

The dry, semi-desertic regions of Baja California, the long peninsula that extends into the Pacific Ocean, and those of the northern uplands have steppes with xerophilous plants. Cacti (including the famous candelabrum-shaped ones), yucca, prickly pear, mammilaria and thorny shrubs are all common. The greener Altiplano Central areas are covered with woods of Scots pine, coniferous plants of various types and oak. In the south is the tropical forest with palms, cedars, bananas, tree-like ferns and orchids, the whole entangled in liane. Endemic plants are the sapodilla (chicle) which produces a latex, used among other things to make chewing gum, and the ceiba, a majestic tree with smooth grey bark. The mostly swampy Tabasco lowlands have vast areas of humid tropical forest while dry forests and savannah are predominant in Yucatán.

The fauna again faithfully reflects the remarkable geographic and orographical position of Mexico. Because there is no true ecological barrier, the fauna has been able to settle all over the country.

Bears, lynx, wolves, coyote, beaver and deer live side by side with jaguars, pumas, tapirs, armadillos, anteaters and monkeys. The lagoons and swamps are home to alligators, turtles, iguana and 267 different amphibians. The numerous bird species (1,424) include cormorants, pelicans, wild geese, herons, flamingoes, 50 different humming-birds

16 Mexico City, Museo Nacional de Antropología. Noble expression of Mayan art, this architectural piece, coming from the Pyramid of the Magician at Uxmal, was made in Puuc style between 650 and 950. It represents the crowned head of a priest emerging from the jaws of a serpent. The stone-work is admirable, appearing almost engraved.

17 Xalapa, Veracruz. Museo de Antropología de la Universidad Veracruzana. This small pottery statue of excellent manufacture comes from the province of Paso de Ovejas, on the coast of the Gulf of Mexico. It is an important example of Totonac art, which flourished around 500 A.D. Here the representation of the costume, jewellery and headgear is precise and highly realistic.

and many migratory birds. Nor is there a shortage of reptiles (685) such as the powerful boa constrictor, capable of growing to a length of 20 feet, and highly poisonous rattlesnakes, of which there are 13 species.

Forty-four national parks, 2 marine parks and 24 biosphere reserves for a total area of almost 20 million acres have been set up to protect this important natural heritage. With a good pair of binoculars and a great deal of patience birds, amphibians and whales can be observed along the coasts and near the lagoons and estuaries. The states of Sinaloa, Baja California, Guerrero, Nayarit, Chiapas, Tabasco and Yucatán in particular are full of nature parks and reserves. The jungles of Quintana Roo, Chiapas and Veracruz are more difficult to penetrate.

A few days should be set aside for expeditions to the Chihuahua Sierra in the state of Durango and the deserts of the north to admire the pumas and lynx. And a stop must be planned to see the whales passing off the coast of Baja California in winter and, between November and March, the 250 million Monarch butterflies that travel from Canada to the El Rosario reserve in the state of Michoácan, close to the Valle de Bravo, west of Mexico City.

There is of course more than this to Mexico: the most intriguing aspect of this country is bound to its civilizations, still cloaked in mystery. The most ancient Mexican settlements date from 20,000 years B.C. These were very probably established by people who took part in the great migrations from Siberia, descending south to America across what is now the Bering Strait: an uninterrupted flow which ended around 8000 B.C. and started prosperous civilizations that built beautiful cities and highly advanced social systems.

In or around 1200 B.C., Central and Southern Mexico saw the rise of the great Olmec civilization; these were the people from the rubber region and they founded major centres such as San Lorenzo (near Acayucan, in the state of Veracruz) which started to develop in 1200 B.C. and La Venta (in the state of Tabasco) which dates from 800 B.C. Most of the Olmec centres grew up on the Gulf of Mexico and these were sacked between 900 and 600 B.C.

Their monumental sculptures, many depicting huge, enigmatic stone faces with grim features, were not discovered until 1939. The Olmecs were responsible for the first organically-structured

18-19 *Yaxchilán, Chiapas. The "City of the green stones" protected by the jungle and a bend of the Río Usumacinta, is in the heart of the Lacandón jungle; three temples in structure similar to those of Palenque form the centre of this Mayan site.*

20-21 *Lake Pátzcuaro, Michoacán. Fishing with the old nets requires great patience and much time but the inhabitants of the small villages built on the water's edge lack neither and continue to live at the pace of times gone by.*

17

civilization and greatly influenced the life and religion of those that followed them. Their major divinities included the were-jaguar, the god of the rain, the plumed snake, the god of fire and the god of maize. In 300 B.C., to the west, on the other side of Mexico, near Oaxaca at Monte Albán, the Zapotec people founded the most highly-populated centre of the period (10,000 inhabitants). A characteristic feature of this civilization are the stone sculptures of Danzantes, sacred dancers whose facial expressions often resemble those of the Olmec heads. What is certain is that the Zapotecs were familiar with the writing and counting of the period.

Together with the Olmecs, they made major artistic, architectural and religious contributions, to be found in all the Mesoamerican cultures. The Mexican stepped pyramid, with a temple on the top, is the fundamental architectural feature. This was where holy ceremonies, social gatherings, sacrifices, ritual games and dances were held.

Although they are compared with the Greeks for their sophisticated astronomical, mathematical and scientific knowledge, with the Romans for their building skills and network of irrigation canals, with the Egyptians for their pyramid-like temples, with the Phoenicians for their excellent sailors and maritime trade, the origin of the Mayas remains a mystery. Historians believe they appeared around the year 1000 B.C.; between 250 B.C. and A.D. 900 the Maya culture reached its maximum splendour and expanded to the Peten (Guatemala) and Yucatán. This was the time of the great temple-pyramids, the sumptuous palaces and the 1,850 miles of roads. Hereditary dynasties, thought to descend from the gods, governed the heavily-populated and wealthy towns (more than 4,000) which stretched from Yucatán to Honduras and were also present in Belize, Guatemala and El Salvador. These centres gave rise to a strong and powerful empire, divided into numerous independent city-states.

Around the beginning of the 16th century A.D., as suddenly as they had appeared, the Maya civilization vanished into thin air for no apparent reason. The archaeologists have differing theories: the over-exploited land had become improductive and the maize crop deified by the Mayas failed; the forest turned into savannah and famines after a population boom, together with plagues, destroyed them. Others hold that they exterminated each other once a system based on political balance between one town and another

had collapsed, much the same as occurred in Italy at the time of the Comunes and Seignories - fraticidal folly condemning them to political and military oblivion. The entire caste of priests apparently committed mass suicide as a dreaded date considered fatal on the holy calendar drew near. The Spanish invasion, in the early 16th century, struck the final blow, although their empire had practically disintegrated decades earlier. This partially saved them from the trauma of the Conquest and the annihilation that caused great bloodshed among the Aztecs and the Incas in Peru.

What is now called the Ruta Maya and is today a highly popular tourist trail was swallowed up by the forest. The temples, palaces, pyramids, astronomical observatories and forts, enveloped in lianes, the roots of huge trees, orchids and ferns, sank into oblivion and all traces of them were lost until the mid-nineteenth century when John Lloyd Stephens, an Amercian lawyer, and Frederick Catherwood, an English illustrator, made two expeditions between 1840 and 1841 and revealed the ancient secrets of the Maya civilzation to the world. A tragic destiny awaited both. Stephens died on 5 October 1852, killed by malarial fever caught in the forest and Catherwood drowned just two years later off the coast of Newfoundland when the steamer *Artic* operating on the London-New York route, was shipwrecked. The implacable curse of the Mayas had reached them.

Common to nearly all the pre-Colombian cultures, but to the Mayas in particular, was what the Spanish called the game of the "pelota" or "ball", more commonly known as Ulama. This is a game of deep religious and sacred significance, imbued with symbolism and ritual. The court represents the world and the path of the ball is that of the Sun and the Moon as they cross the sky, in the ceaseless alternation of night and day, darkness and light. The ball court, the shape of a double T or a Latin capital I was closed on both sides by tiers of seats, for the spectators, resting on a platform made of walls 25 feet high. In the centre of each, near the top, was a ring in carved stone depicting Quetzalcoatl. The ball struck by the two opposing teams had to pass through these narrow circles, called marcadores. Skilled and foolhardy player-warriors, with a powerful physique, flicked the ball with their hips. The losers were sacrificed to the gods although some scholars venture to suggest that it was the winner who was sacrificed.

The ball was made of hule, or caoutchouc. This white latex is obtained by cutting into the

tree called *castilloa elástica* or ulequahitl, which
in the Nahuatl tongue means hule tree.
The chicleros, those still familiar with the secrets
of processing hule, mix it with juice from another
plant, the Machaguana or *Operculia Rhodocalyx*,
heating the mixture with firebrands until the paste
slowly solidifies, becoming elastic and a
brownish-gold caramel colour. It is a long,
complex and extremely difficult process. In this
mysterious alchemy of primeval elements, hule
means constant movement. Almost as if by magic,
the liquid is turned into a ball that bounces,
shoots through the air, bounding from one side
to the other, endowed with an uncontrollable,
irrepressible vitality. The game of Ulama played
a particularly important role in pre-Colombian
cultures, representing a sort of religious rite.
In a certain sense it allows the visual and concrete
sanctification of the contest between the forces
of light and darkness. The pelota was nearly always
the size of a human skull, the religious and
metaphysical significance being clear. The head is
the centre of man's vitality, the seat of reason
through which man observes and knows the
world. It forms a relationship with the
supernatural and the divine.

In Central Mexico, when the Maya farther
south were at the height of their splendour around
the third century A.D., the city of Teotihuacán
became a religious, political and trading centre.
Designed to a complex urban plan, it was a major
and powerful metropolis inhabited by
approximately 200,000 people. Works and
commerce, good government and peaceful
relations with its neighbours, control of the trade
routes between the Pacific and the Gulf of Mexico
and those descending from the north to the south
of the country gave it a stable prosperity.
The huge pyramids were conceived with the use
of the talud and the tablero, respectively sloping
and horizontal sections. City of peace and trade,
its vast dominions reached as far as Guatemala and
were not rigidly presided over by any army.
"The ponderous pyramids of San Juan Teotihuaca,
the House of Quetzalcoatl wreathed with the
snake of all snakes, his huge fangs white and pure
to-day as in the lost centuries when his makers
were alive. He has not died. He is not so dead
as the Spanish churches, this all-enwreathing
dragon of the horror of Mexico" wrote D.H.
Lawrence in his novel. In antiquity, Teotihuacán
was second in size only to Rome. It was the capital
of an empire that expanded for more than a
thousand years in the centre of the central
Mexican uplands. Its palaces, pyramids, architects,
artists and merchants were just as good as those

*22-23 Guadalajara, Jalisco.
Charreadas, sombreros, rodeos, tequila,
mariachis, lassoes and stomping horses
all are part of the local tradition.
The* Palenque *is held here in June and
October and the most skilled and expert
horsemen from all over the state gather
for this lively festival. As well as the
men, seductive young girls compete
in rash and dangerous manoeuvres,
the expression of a culture and tradition
bound to the land and cattle and horse
breeding. Splendid costumes are worn
for the occasion by men and women
alike: high leather boots, skintight, soft
leather trousers, embroidered shirts
and wide sombreros. The women don
brightly coloured outfits with flounced
skirts down to the ground decorated
with lace and ribbons.*

of Rome, the makers of empires. Like ancient Egypt, Teotihuacán is still an unexplained mystery. Its majestic pyramids were based on the movement of the stars. Suddenly, all this disappeared with the rise of tougher nomad peoples pressing down from the north and it had to capitulate. Teotihuacán was destroyed around 600 A.D. and was succeeded by the Aztecs. These were a nomad people who came to the Mexican uplands from California in the twelfth century and in 1325 founded Tenochtitlán, where Mexico City now stands. At its height, the Aztec empire stretched from the Gulf of Mexico to the Pacific. Its power was based on efficient public administration, an influential priesthood and a permanent, strong and well-equipped army. Towns flourished together with trade and agriculture. A warrior people by inclination, little given over to artistic exploration, the Aztecs adopted the basic elements of the Teotihuacán and Tollán cultures. Their art, whether architecture or sculpture, always has a grandiose and colossal imprint. The capital had stone palaces with cedarwood roofs that were furnished with paintings and rugs. When the Spanish arrived they found a well-organized and powerful empire.

"Before the Spaniards arrived, ten years earlier, an ill omen appeared in the sky, like a tongue of fire, an aurora. It seemed to rain tiny drops, as if the sky were splitting; it expanded at the base, and narrowed as it rose. To the middle of the sky, to the heart of the heavens it reached, into the innermost depths of the sky it penetrated. In such a manner it was seen, towards the East it showed itself, shining in the dead of night. Day seemed to come and later the Sun dissolved it. When it appeared, the people would start to wail, beating their mouths, they were dismayed, all work would cease". Thus records the Florentine Code, faithfully reproducing the mysterious circumstances, the agonizing wait for imminent wonders and the sudden arrival of strange people from the immense expanse of the Ocean.

Popocatépetl, now inactive, looms above Cholula and produced a spectacular lava flow at the beginning of 1519, just before the arrival of Cortés. The Aztec emperor Montezuma sent ten observers to the top. Only two returned.

Hernán Cortés left Cuba on 15 February 1519 and landed at Cozumel, where he met Jerónimo de Aguilar, who had been shipwrecked several years earlier on the Caribbean coast and had made friends with the natives. From here Cortés and his men moved along the coast of the Gulf of Mexico, going ashore close to today's

Veracruz. Here he made a fatal encounter with La Malinche, a native princess who became his highly-valued companion. After about three months he headed inland and in just a few years managed to overcome the Aztecs thanks to his fire-arms, the use of horses, the alliances he established with the tribes hostile to the Aztecs and omens interpreted by Montezuma as meaning that he was the long-awaited "blonde god". Not until 1547 however did the Spanish manage to subjugate most of the country. In 1535 Spain appointed a viceroy and favoured Spanish immigration. The Church did the rest through a vast and determined operation of evangelization of the Indians, building 10,000 churches and as many monasteries in the space of a century. The Indians were the victims of an out and out genocide: by 1570 more than 12 million had died. This number was to rise in the following decades to over 25 million.

They were wiped out by the new diseases introduced by the conquistadores and by forced labour, to which they were mainly subjected in the mines, and condemned to the stake for being pagans and "children of the devil".

Bad Spanish government, the policy of pillage and racial segregation, the new ideas that were coming from France after the 1789 revolution and from North America, following its newly-won freedom, the growing tension between the criollos and the Spanish born in the motherland, all accelerated the process of independence. Much of the clergy sided with the patriots, convinced of the need for social reforms, the abolition of slavery, exemption from taxes and agricultural reform. It was the parish priest Miguel Hidalgo who sparked off the fight for independence. At 5 a.m. on 16 September 1810 in the small town of Dolores, Hidalgo rang the bells of the church of Señora de los Dolores calling the Mexicans to battle and issuing El Grito, the cry against the exploitation by the gachupines, the great land owners who were starving the peasants. Independence was declared in 1821 although it was not really achieved until 1824 and the first federal constitution. Troubled and dramatic times followed. There were 34 changes of government between 1821 and 1854, when the dictator Antonio López de Santa Ana fell from power.

Many wars were fought. 1846 saw the explosion of the conflict between Mexico and the United States, the latter having taken over Texas. Defeated two years later, the Mexicans were forced to hand over California and New Mexico.

24 top Oaxaca. The church of Santo Domingo with its splendid baroque façade is perhaps the most spectacular in all Mexico. On the carved wooden ceiling at the entrance is Santo Domingo's family tree. The church interior is lavishly adorned with paintings, bas-reliefs and gilded altars; the Rosary chapel houses an 18th-century statue of Our Lady. The cloister of the adjacent Dominican monastery, erected in 1570, is now a Regional Museum. It conserves important evidence of the State's history after the Spanish conquest and numerous objects from Monte Albán, including the precious relics from Tomb no. 7: gold masks, jade, amber and turquoise jewellery.

24 bottom Izamal, Yucatán. The monastery of San Antonio de Padua was built by the Franciscans between 1553 and 1561 using the material from the demolished Mayan temple dedicated to the god Kinich Kakmó. The great courtyard of the complex extends over 9,500 square yards and is circumscribed by a slightly arched portico, interrupted only by the façade of the sanctuary of the Virgen de Izamal. Its single-nave interior houses a statue of the Madonna, patron saint of Yucatán, and a Black Christ. A short distance from the village are the remains of eleven pyramids, now little more than piles of rubble.

25 *Oaxaca. The 17th-century church of La Soledad is a major example of Mexican baroque. Inside it houses the statue of the Virgen de la Soledad, the patron saint of the city. Founded in 1486 by the Aztecs and point of encounter of the various pre-Colombian populations in ancient times, it practically became a personal possession of Cortés as Charles V assigned him extensive properties in this very region and the title of Marqués del Valle de Oaxaca: he was responsible for the numerous Dominican monasteries that still exist. Capital of the state of the same name, where Benito Juaréz and Porfirio Díaz were born, it has not allowed progress to make a significant impact: it has just over 250,000 inhabitants and modern buildings remain a rare sight. The city, all perpendicular streets, is a succession of low houses with large windows and wrought iron railings.*

26-27 *Zacatecas. The capital of the state of the same name - which comes from the Aztec words* zacatl, *grass, and* tlan, *place - grew in 1548 from the agglomeration of huts belonging to those trying to take the silver from the Zacateco Indians, the first inhabitants of the region. The wealth from the mines contributed to the prosperity of the zone and buildings and sumptuous churches were soon built; the most outstanding is the Cathedral (at the centre of the photograph) erected in 1612 and finished in 1752 which became one of the grandest in the country.*

28-29 *San Cristóbal de las Casas, Chiapas. Situated at a height of 7,419 feet, this town was founded in 1528 and has maintained its austere charm intact. Of its numerous monasteries and rich noble homes the most striking is the large baroque Cathedral, erected in 1528, demolished in the 17th century and rebuilt in 1696.*

This amounted to practically half of the country. A bloody civil war erupted in 1858 after the approval of the democratic constitution. It was won by the liberal Benito Pablo Juárez, a Zapotec Indian, and in 1861 he came to power. Britain, France and Spain rose up against him under the pretext of collecting the considerable foreign debts run up by the country. The British and Spanish withdrew a year later but the French embarked upon a disastrous adventure. At first they were highly successful and managed to install Maximilian of Hapsburg in Mexico City as Emperor in 1864. Juárez however obtained the support of the United States who convinced the French to withdraw their troops. Maximilian was captured and executed by firing squad at Querétaro. Juárez again became president, remaining thus until 1872.

He was succeeded by Porfirio Díaz, a very clever man of mixed blood, who controlled the country for thirty years. A dictator to all effects, he opened Mexico to foreign investment: 40% of US capital was tied up in these regions, concessions were made with no recompense and the mines were worked without the payment of taxes. In this way he condemned most Mexicans to total poverty.

In 1910, an umpteenth election fraud on the part of the dictator Díaz and the gaoling of Madero, the official candidate, caused the inevitable explosion of the revolution, a heroic exploit which in ten years swept the entire country towards democracy. The leading figures were the campesinos, the poor landless peasants, and the liberal intellectuals.

In 1911 the Porfiriato era officially came to an end when Díaz was thrown out of office. The battle raged in the countryside under the guidance of prestigious leaders: Emiliano Zapata, Pancho Villa and Alvaro Obregón. The civil war did not end until 1920. The revolution started a number of radical reforms that put the country in step with the times. A new reformist constitution was enacted in 1917. The mines were nationalized and the large estates expropriated, giving rise to agricultural reform. Today the Estados Unitos Mexicanos are a federal, presidential republic of 31 states and one federal district, which comprises the capital, Mexico City. Every state has considerable autonomy, each with its own Governor, elected assembly and constitution. The PRI, the Partido Revolucionario Istitucional, in power since the Twenties, still rules the country.

In the public imagination Mexico is not just nature and great civilization, it is, above all,

an explosive mix of ingredients: the remains of colonialism, the mariachi (street musicians with large sombreros that sing romantic love songs), sun, beaches, tequila (an alcoholic drink that sets the mouth on fire), the Indians, the señoritas with their dark, languishing eyes and the muchachos muy machos with their shiny, sleeked hair: a fascinating Mexico waiting to be discovered.

The journey starts from the capital, Mexico City, the "monster-city" with 20 million inhabitants; the largest megalopolis in the world, it has many surprises in store: the finest museum of pre-Hispanic cultures, that of Anthropology; the works of the most famous mural artists conserved in various museums; the homes, now museums, very close to one another in the Coyoacán district, of two rivals: Leon Trotsky, one of the fathers of Communism who fled here from Stalin's henchmen, out to kill him, and Frida Kahlo, the well-known Mexican artist.

One after the other to the north lie the main Ciudades Coloniales, founded by the conquistadores from the mid-sixteenth century onwards. Noble palaces, monasteries and splendid cathedrals carved by the Indians in the style in vogue in Spain at the the time give a wonderful insight into New Spain. In Tepotztlán, the monastery of San Francesco Saverio is a fine example of colonial art.

Querétaro, with the impressive arches of the eighteenth-century aqueduct; San Miguel de Allende, a Baroque gem; Guanajuato and its silver mines; Morelia, its centre dominated by the cathedral; Guadalajara, with its charros, the reckless Mexican cowboys; Zacatecas, its palaces and churches embellished during the Churrigueresque frenzy - an all-Mexican architectural style top-heavy in decoration and friezes. All of these are magnificent and precious splendours of a bewitching land.

Mysterious civilizations
waiting to be discovered

30 top *Palenque, Chiapas.*
Rediscovered at the beginning of the last century, after having been abandoned for hundreds of years, Palenque was one of the most important Mayan holy cities. Inhabited from the 1st century A.D., it rose to prominence between 600 and 800; in architectural terms it represents a fundamental step in the history of this ancient civilization. It was constructed on a series of artificial terraces on the foothills of the Chiapas sierra, in the middle of the jungle, around a nucleus of palaces and temples that show a remarkable elegance and considerable compositional taste.
Among the most important monuments in the archaeological area (which comprises a small part of the city's original extension) is what is called the "Northern Group" consisting of a number of religious buildings aligned on a massive embankment and reached by climbing grand flights of steps.

30 bottom *Kabah, Yucatán.*
The name of this ancient Mayan town not far from Uxmal means "the chiselling hand". The most impressive monument here is Codz Poop (literally "furled mat") a grandiose, multistorey building dedicated to Chac, the rain god, its façade being adorned with many masks.

31 *Mexico City, Museo Nacional de Antropología. This splendid stone mask, covered with a mosaic in turquoise, red shells, mother of pearl and obsidian, belongs to the Teotihuacán style of the so-called third phase and dates from the 5th century A.D.*

Chichén Itza, the ancient capital of Yucatán

32 left *Chichen Itza, Yucatán. After having been a major Mayan city, after the Toltec invasion (i.e. around the end of the 10th century A.D.),Chichén Itza became the most important city in Yucatán and soon grew to vast proportions.*
The local monuments are an eloquent sign of the fusion of the Mayan building techniques and the pompous style brought by the invaders: a good example is the Nunnery, a splendid building literally covered with decorations, bas reliefs and angular sculptures that obsessively repropose the representation of the rain god, portrayed with a menacing expression and characteristic long, rolled-up nose.

32-33 *Chichén Itza, Yucatán.*
El Castillo, a pyramid on 9 levels and 79 feet high, is the most important building in this ancient Mayan city. The sanctuary proper - consecrated to the god Kukulcán - is on the top of the structure, reached up 4 flights of steps, one on each side: each has 91 steps which added to the platform on the top make a total of 365, equal to the number of days in the year. The remarkable ability of the Mayan astronomers is also demonstrated by the "descent of the god Quetzalcoatl Kukulcán to the earth": every 21 March, the spring equinox, the rays of the setting sun project the changing shadows of the nine levels on the side of the main stairway (to the left of the picture), adorned at the bottom with two serpent heads, and produce an extraordinary optical effect by which a huge serpent seems to be moving from the top of the pyramid down towards the ground.

34-35 *Chichén Itzá, Yucatan.*
The Temple of the Warriors takes its name from the images sculpted in bas-relief on the internal pillars of the top sanctuary; this pyramid on three levels clearly reveals the influence of Toltec style. The building is surrounded by numerous pillars and columns that used to support the roofs of long meeting halls.

35 top *Chichén Itza, Yucatán.*
The building known as the Nunnery was given this unusual name for the large number of rooms it has, like a convent. In actual fact it must have been a holy building connected with the cult of the god Chac, the lord of the rain.

35 top centre *Chichén Itza, Yucatán.*
El Caracol is certainly the most famous Mayan astronomical observatory. Its name, which means conch shell, comes from the internal staircase that led to a room with seven rectangular windows; from here the priests observed the movements of the stars in order to plan their predictions rituals. It is a two-storey building 39 feet high placed on an equal number of square-plan bases one on top of the other; its round form is an exception in Mayan architecture and was probably imported by the Toltecs from central Mexico.

35 centre bottom *Chichén Itza, Yucatán. The Ossuary, otherwise known as the High Priest's Grave, is a pyramid with a wide flight of steps leading to the top. The remains of a high priest were found together with other human bones and numerous precious objects during excavations in a natural cave below the building and reached via a carefully concealed vertical well.*

35 bottom *Chichén Itza, Yucatán The Mayan cities all had at least one ball court used for the ritual game of* pelota, *played by two teams who had to hit a ball made of caoutchouc through two stone rings fixed to the high lateral walls without using their hands. The Chichén Itza court, 183 yards long, is the largest in Mesoamerica: the relief decorations - which also depict the decapitation of a player - highlight the cruel side of the culture imported by the Toltecs and their familiarity with human sacrifice, little practised by the Mayans.*

Uxmal, a treasure in Puuc style

36-37 *Uxmal, Yucatán.*
This sumptuous and immense city, the largest Mayan urban centre, is thought to represent the absolute height of Puuc architectural style, which here attained an exceptional stylistic refinement. Distinctive features are the mainly horizontal development of the structures, elongated linearity and the orderly sequence of the reliefs, the finely decorated panels and the custom of leaving the lower part of the buildings devoid of decoration - all elements that can be observed in the Nunnery Quadrangle.

37 top *Uxmal, Yucatán.*
The Governor's Palace is almost unanimously considered the loveliest building in classic Mayan architecture, both for its harmonious proportions and the magnificent decorations. Extremely well conserved despite its remarkable size - approximately 110 yards long - it stands on a number of large terraces south of the Pyramid of the Magician; the building has a central block and two minor side parts, divided by two high, narrow passages with a mock vault; the long sequence of rooms inside would suggest that it was used for administration purposes.

37 centre *Uxmal, Yucatán.*
The Nunnery Quadrangle - the name was given by the Spanish conquerors for its resemblance to a cloister - is a complex consisting of four buildings not connected to one another and set around a large square courtyard. There are 74 rooms in all, built on different levels. The northern building, preceded by a long flight of steps is decorated with fasciae bearing geometrical motifs, stylized huts and masks of the god Chac.

37 bottom *Uxmal, Yucatán.*
The Nunnery Quadrangle (left) and the Pyramid of the Magician (right) emerge from the lush tropical forest. The Pyramid, one of the most unusual in Mayan architecture, is the result of five construction phases which lasted from the 6th to the 10th centuries. On the top there are two separate temples built on two levels in different styles and reached up very steep flights of steps placed on the east and west sides.

38-39 *Uxmal, Yucatán.*
The image of the god Chac is omnipresent in the Nunnery Quadrangle: the terrifying Mayan realism was conceived to provoke terror and respect for the divinity, so that the followers would unconditionally accept the words of the priests, the only intermediaries between the people and the gods.

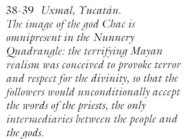

Bonampak, images from the past

40 *Mexico City, Museo Nacional de Antropología. Because of their fragility and the tropical climate, most of the wall paintings that adorned the holy buildings of the Mayan cities have been lost; nonetheless, the few that have survived demonstrate the remarkable technical and compositional skills of the Mayan craftsmen. Of particular significance are frescoes found in three rooms in the Temple of*

Paintings at Bonampak, in the State of Chiapas, and reproduced in the Museo de Antropología in Mexico City; room 2 - seen in this picture - was dedicated to battles and filled with hundreds of characters.

41 *Mexico City, Museo Nacional de Antropología. This photograph also shows a detail of room 2 in the Temple of the Paintings at Bonampak; the name literally*

means "painted wall". Seen here are some armed noble Mayan warriors and a group of prisoners, one bleeding copiously. The unknown Mayan painters were able to turn scenes of everyday life, war and celebration into pictures of exceptional vivacity and descriptive detail using a vast range of colours: unfortunately many of the hieroglyphics and writing that accompanied the paintings have not yet been deciphered.

Masterpieces in stone
in the name of Chac

42 top left *Kabah, Yucatán.*
The façade of Codz Poop, a splendid
example of what is called "Mayan
baroque", is decorated with more than
three hundred long-nosed masks of the
god Chac arranged in prominent, long
horizontal and vertical rows. Nowhere
else in Yucatán, except for Uxmal, did
Puuc decorative style become so
elaborate and insistent.

42 top right *Xlapak, Yucatán.*
Immersed in the dense tropical forest, this
archaeological site is neither well known
nor much visited - a fact that tends to
increase its fascination. The
archaeological area contains buildings
in characteristic Puuc style, the most
interesting being the Royal Palace,
as always adorned with the recurring
effigy of the god Chac.

42 bottom left *Sayil, Yucatán.*
The spectacular building known as El
Palacio, almost 217 yards long and set
on three tiers, is one of the greatest
accomplishments of Mayan
architecture. This colossal structure,
which seems to have been derived from
the traditional stepped pyramid, shows
the successful application of the column,
a distinctive feature of Puuc style.

42-43 *Kabah, Yucatán. Codz Poop*
stands on a large artificial platform
reached via a flight of steps. The obsessive
presence of the mask of the god Chac on
the façade of the building had a distinct
propitiatory significance as rainfall is
immensely important in this region. The
construction of the Kabah monuments,
as for the other sites nearby (Sayil,
Xlapak, Labná), dates from a period
between the 8th and the 13th centuries.

Tulum, a stronghold on the coast

44-45 *Tulum, Quintana Roo.*
This Mayan city - the name means
"stronghold" - is one of the few
overlooking the Caribbean sea and the
only one to have been systematically
explored. Similar to a fortress and
surrounded by a circuit of walls, it was
an outpost of great strategic importance
for the control of trade along a large
stretch of the coast. Dedicated to the
"descending or diving god - probably the
setting sun - it appeared in the second
half of the 6th century A.D.
One of the main buildings within the
archaeological boundary is El Castillo,
a temple-fortress built above the sea; its
columns are decorated with serpents.
Tulum has the unmistakable
appearance of a fortified stronghold,
emphasized by massive and not very
refined, indeed coarse, architecture in
which defence is the primary function;
despite this its favourable position makes
it particularly charming.

45 top *Tulum, Quintana Roo.*
The most famous monument in this
ancient fortified city is the Temple of the
Frescoes; some fairly well-preserved
murals can still be seen inside: some
show Chac and Ixchel, the goddess of the
moon, others the three realms of the
Mayan universe (that of the deceased,
that of the living, that of the gods).

45 bottom *Tulum, Quintana Roo.*
El Castillo is the product of numerous
additions and reconstructions:
originally it must have appeared as a
simple worshipping platform on which
was built a rectangular-plan palace
topped with a temple reached up a flight
of steps. A stele dating from 564 A.D.
was found in the Temple of the Initial
Series, to its right, and is now on display
in the British Museum in London.

Palenque, a city re-emerges from the forest

46 top *Palenque, Chiapas. Palenque is thought by many to be the core of the Mayan "mystery": it was in fact here more than elsewhere that their civilization slowly faded away for no apparent reason, allowing nature to take possession of their extraordinary monuments. The site now covers a fairly small area, no more than 600 yards per side, but the archaeological area plunges more than 4 miles into the forest. The city - inhabited from the 1st century A.D. onwards but which flourished between 600 and 800 - is one of the most important centres of the classical period, both for its grandiose architectural complexes and its distinctive rich ornamentation in plaster and stone. The picture shows the Temple of the Sun (to the fore, left) and the Temple of the Inscriptions (to the rear, right).*

46 bottom *Palenque, Chiapas. This photograph shows the Temple of the Sun (left) and the Temple of the Cross (right); both structures feature a typical Mayan architectural and decorative element, the "roofcomb", a high, elaborate plastered crest placed at the top of roofs. The Temple of the Sun owes its name to a splendid, sculpted slab, found in the sanctuary, depicting the worship of the sun god. The Temple of the Cross, the tallest building in Palenque, was named for a panel decorated with historical scenes and a symbol that resembles a cross - its meaning is still the object of debate - placed above a mask and flanked by two priests.*

46-47 *Palenque, Chiapas. The Temple of Inscriptions, dated 7th century A.D., is a pyramid 69 feet high, the most majestic construction in Palenque even though the rich roofcomb that adorned it has been lost. The temple on the top opens onto the square through a portico with four pillars, embellished with stucco reliefs. In 1952 the Mexican archaeologist Alberto Ruz Lhuillier found a passageway beneath the floor of the sanctuary leading to an underground crypt that contained the sarcophagus of a king-priest, Pakal, surrounded by a rich array of funeral objects in jade: it was a sensational discovery, unique in the history of Mayan architecture.*

48 top left *Palenque, Chiapas.*
The Palace is the largest and most articulated complex in Palenque: the various buildings stand on an artificial platform 32 feet high, 328 long and 262 wide. The constructions are arranged around four inner courtyards and are linked by a veritable maze of corridors and passages.

48 bottom left *Palenque, Chiapas.*
The tower that dominates the Palace (to the left of the picture) is unique in Mayan architecture: having a square plan and four storeys high it was probably used as an astronomical observatory. The Mayan priests had developed amazing mathematical and cosmological knowledge and had even correctly calculated the movement of Venus and the duration of the year with an approximation of error smaller than that of the Gregorian calendar.

48 right *Palenque, Chiapas.*
Inside the Palace are many bas-reliefs portraying noblemen, priests and warriors. The Mayan society was very much controlled by those in positons of power: at the top were the priests, trustees of astronomical and mathematical knowledge; they alone could legitimate the political power of the belligerent aristocracy which was on the second "rung" of the social ladder.
Lower down came the merchants who guaranteed contacts betwen the various city-states; the common people, mainly peasants and craftsmen, were totally submissive.
For the Mayan priests knowledge was applied science and familiarity with the natural phenomena used for the common good, rather than abstract speculation. This explains the total devotion that the people had for them.

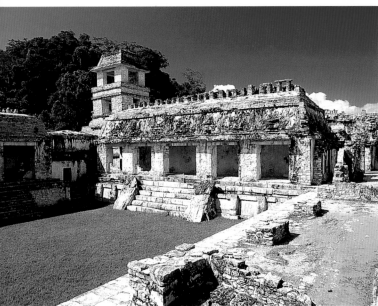

48-49 *Palenque, Chiapas.*
The Temple of the Count is screened by luxuriant, age-old trees. A steep stairway leads to the sanctuary on the top made up of two parallel rooms that overlook the exterior through the customary pillared portico.
Unfortunately the temple has lost its roofcomb and the whole pyramid has greatly suffered from the ravages of time. Abandoned for reasons unknown before the arrival of the Conquerors, Palenque was soon overgrown with vegetation and sank into oblivion; it was not rediscovered until the first half of the last century. The end of the Maya civilization remains an enigma: some believe that its decline was caused by a population explosion and a terrible famine, others speak of a fatal plague and still others of a war between cities conducted to total extermination.

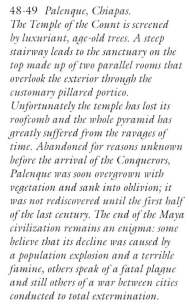

Mitla,
the city of stone frets

50-51 *Mitla, Oaxaca. Founded in the 9th century A.D. by the Mixtecs, the original inhabitants of the region, Mitla later came under the Zapotecs from an area slightly farther south. The town is thus the result of a particularly successful cultural and artistic fusion, the former population being more occupied with everyday problems and the latter devoted to the glorification of the gods. The religious buildings of Mitla are always incorporated into secular structures and are far less ostentatious than the temples erected, for instance, by the Zapotecs at Monte Albán. The five surviving groups of buildings, all constructed to a quadrilateral plan are of extreme constructional and artistic quality, the latter being seen in the large wall panels of mosaics in relief made with small pieces of calcareous stone painstakingly arranged in 14 variations on the theme of the Greek key. A true masterpiece is the Hall of the Columns, seen here; the name comes from the long hall just inside the porticoed entrance and originally supported by six columns.*
The walls of this splendid monument are covered with countless rows of mosaics showing rigorous plastic creativity and geometrical division of space that are the result of skilful mathematical calculations.

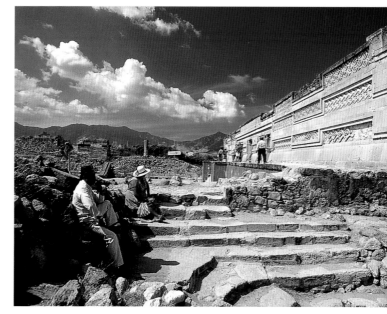

Monte Albán, the city of the gods

52-53 *Monte Albán, Oaxaca. Having settled in south-west Mexico around the year 1000 B.C., the Zapotecs rose to their maximum splendour between the 3rd and the 10th century A.D.; their capital - known today as Monte Albán - stood on high ground above what is now Oaxaca. Constructed entirely on an artificial platform and organized around a large central square, in turn surrounded by numerous temples, at one stage it had a population of approximately 10,000 inhabitants. The architecture of this city consecrated to the worship of the gods features buildings of austere composition and precise geometric volumes. One is Building IV, a pyramid which used to have a temple on the top.*

53 top right *Monte Albán, Oaxaca. The Zapotecs gave a considerable artistic, architectural and religious impulse to the subsequent Mexican cultures. The stepped pyramid, in particular, crowned with a temple, later widely used by the Aztecs, seems to have been inherited from them. The photograph, taken from the top of Building IV, shows the huge North Platform on which stand numerous holy buildings.*

53 centre right *Monte Albán, Oaxaca. The* pelota *ball court is very well conserved; the losers were apparently sacrificed to the gods in this sort of cerimonial duel - Ullamaliztli - that shocked Hernán Cortés himself. It is very hard to understand the true significance of the human sacrifices that were part of the religious rites of all the pre-Colombian civilizations.*

53 bottom right *Monte Albán, Oaxaca. The slabs in bas-relief portraying the* danzantes *are typical of the Zapotec civilization: although these characters appear to be lost in their sacred dance the exact meaning is still unclear.*

54-55 *Monte Albán, Oaxaca. This aerial picture shows the two complexes at the centre of the large square: the building to the left, one of the oldest on the site, is thought to have been the first astronomical observatory of Mesoamerica.*

Teotihuacán:
the metropolis of great pyramids

56 *Teotihuacán, Estado de México. Coming from the north at the beginning of the 13th century and settling in the Valley of Mexico, the Aztecs gradually wiped out the local populations until by the mid 15th century they had created a vast empire. Yet, when the Aztecs settled on Lake Texcoco and started to construct their capital, Tenochtitlán (now Mexico City) they were not far from the ruins of what had already been the largest city in Mesoamerica: the* remarkable *Teotihuacán, founded in the 1st century A.D. and prosperous for 700 years before being destroyed by events still for the most part unknown. At the time of its utmost splendour this metropolis had a population of 250,000 inhabitants. Situated in a strategic position that allowed it to control trade towards the Gulf of Mexico, it gradually changed from a farming town into a trading centre and manufacturer of objects in obsidian,* produced in its workshops; with the economical and social growth of the city came increasingly monumental religious buildings, set along a thoroughfare known as the Avenue of the Dead. This aerial picture shows the centre of the archaeological site, dominated by the huge Pyramid of the Moon. Built on a base of 163 by 152 yards and on four levels this artificial mountain is 150 feet high, 32 less than in the past.*

57 Teotihuacán, Estado de México.
Even more impressive than the Pyramid
of the Moon - and better conserved - is the
Pyramid of the Sun which rises on the east
side of the Avenue of the Dead. Considered
one of man's greatest works in antiquity,
it is constructed on a square base of 246
yards per side and is on five levels; today
it stands 206 feet high but it is thought to
have been 39 feet higher when the great
temple still stood on its summit. It has
been calculated that 3 million tons of stone
were used to build it. Some years ago, at
the foot of the great flight of steps,
archaeologists discovered a well leading to
a tunnel, a hundred or so yards long with
plastered walls, and a cave divided into
four rooms beneath the great structure.
This was probably an underground
sanctuary but, as for the whole city and
its elusive inhabitants, the mystery has
not yet been totally solved. The Pyramid
of the Sun, like that of the Moon, is
surrounded by large platforms (used for
the celebration of religious rites), similar
to those seen to the fore of the picture.

The museums
of wonders

58 top left *Mexico City, Museo Nacional de Antropología. A life-size reconstruction of the tomb of the king-priest Pakal, discovered in the depths of the Temple of the Inscriptions in Palenque, displays the rich sarcophagus and funeral objects.*

58 top right *Mexico City, Museo Nacional de Antropología. This Mayan incense carrier portraying the god of the rain Chac-mool and made in finely-shaped, polychrome pottery was found at Mayapán: it dates from the post classical period (900-1500 A.D.).*

58 bottom right *Mexico City, Museo Nacional de Antropología. A warrior is depicted in this Mayan terracotta statuette dating from the classical period (250 B.C. - 900 A.D.).*

59 *Mexico City, Museo Nacional de Antropología. The stone disc from Chinkultic, a refined Mayan work of art dated 590 A.D., shows a player of Ulama - the sacred ball game. The ball used for this game was made with caoutchouc - in the Mayan tongue known as* hule *- obtained by tapping the trunk of the* Castilloa elastica. *The* chicleros, *the craftsmen who knew all the secrets of* hule *processing, mixed the white latex with juice obtained from another plant, the* Operculia rhodocalyx, *heating the whole with firebrands until the mixture gradually solidified, gaining elasticity and a golden brown colour. The incredible speed of the ball, its response to the blows of the players and capacity to soar high in the air inside the court in honour of the gods all depended on the skill of the* chicleros.

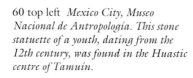

60 top left *Mexico City, Museo Nacional de Antropología. This stone statuette of a youth, dating from the 12th century, was found in the Huastic centre of Tamuín.*

60 top right *Mexico City, Museo Nacional de Antropología. Found at Monte Albán and dated 200 A.D., this terracotta votive urn is a typical example of the Zapotec civilization, which evolved between the 5th century B.C. and the Spanish conquest in the central valleys of Oaxaca. These people called themselves Ben Zaa ("the People of the Clouds") and were basically devoted to the cultivation of maize. They gave rise to an extremely refined artistic and architectural heritage.*

60 bottom *Mexico City, Museo Nacional de Antropología. This earthenware Zapotec urn portrays a man with outstretched arms; it comes from tomb number 113 on Monte Albán. As well as the headgear adorned with the symbol of the jaguar, an animal thought to be sacred, the man is also wearing a rich breastpiece.*

61 *Oaxaca, Museo Regional. This splendid gold breastpiece depicting a warrior with calendar symbols on his bodice belongs to the Mixtec culture. The jewel was found in tomb number 7 on Monte Albán and dates from the time when the ancient Zapotec worshipping centre had been turned into a Mixtec necropolis.*

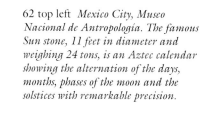

62 top left *Mexico City, Museo Nacional de Antropología. The famous Sun stone, 11 feet in diameter and weighing 24 tons, is an Aztec calendar showing the alternation of the days, months, phases of the moon and the solstices with remarkable precision.*

62 top right *Villahermosa, Tabasco. The local regional museum of archaeology contains many Mayan relics from the late classical period (200-900 A.D.). An outstanding piece is this anthropomorphic incense carrier in pottery and richly decorated with elegant plastic motifs.*

62 bottom *Mexico City, Museo Nacional de Antropología. This stone statue, an admirable specimen of Aztec sculpture, shows a priest bearing the emblems of the god of fire.*

63 *Mexico City Museo Nacional de Antropología. This funeral mask is one of the rarest and most precious pieces of Mayan art. Decorated in mosaic with large pieces of jade, it covered the face of the king Pakal whose sepulchre was hidden in the Temple of the Inscriptions in Palenque.*

64 top *Mexico City, Museo Nacional de Antropología. Of exquisite manufacture, this mask in polychrome terracotta belongs to the Teotihuacán culture of the third period (2nd-7th century A.D.). It is a highly stylized representation of a man, probably a priest, with two large rings in his ear lobes and one hanging from his nose.*

64 bottom *Teotihuacán, Estado de México. Exhibited in the local museum is this piece of pottery depicting a mythological bird spraying water from its beak. This, together with other similar pieces, was probably part of the decoration on a holy building.*

65 *Teotihuacán, Estado de México.*
This sculpture in stone reproducing the
fearsome head of the god Tlaloc in the
form of a serpent and dating from the
3rd century A.D. comes from the Temple
of Quetzalcóatl, one of the main holy
buildings in the huge pre-Aztec
metropolis.

Baroque harmony and skyscrapers on the sea

66 top *Guadalajara, Jalisco. The city, founded in 1542 and now the capital of the State of Jalisco, has grown beyond measure around the old centre which has a plan similar to a huge Latin cross. Situated at 5,400 feet above sea level, it has more than 4 million inhabitants. The heart of the metropolis is Plaza Mayor on which stands the Palacio de Gobierno, dating from the first half of the 17th century; inside, the main staircase is decorated with a mural by José Clemente Orozco, the famous artist born in Guadalajara.*

66 bottom *Acapulco, Guerrero. Acapulco bay, with its stunning skyscrapers set along the crescent-moon of sand, is one of the most spectacular in all the world. It rose to universal fame in the Fifties when the stars of Hollywood turned it into a floodlit stage for their violent passions; its myth still survives, only slightly tarnished by a frenetic population and construction expansion which in recent years has seen the population grow to almost a million inhabitants.*

67 *Mexico City. The capital spread over 580 square miles at an altitude of 7,347 feet, is home to one tenth of the country's population. Some cold statistical data may give an idea of what "El Monstruo", as this chaotic and vast megalopolis has been nicknamed by the Mexicans, really is. Mexico City is home to 49% of national industries and 38% of its services; 42% of the gross national product is produced here; more than 3,000,000 motor vehicles circulate; every year 5,500,000 tons of polluting substances accumulate in the air and every day it produces 15,000 tons of refuse.*

"El Monstruo", the largest capital in the world

68 top *Mexico City. The Palacio Nacional, a huge building in strictly colonial baroque style, stands on the east side of the Plaza de la Constitución (second in size only to Red Square in Moscow), better known as the Zócalo. The building, which houses the Government and various governmental offices, was built in 1692 on the remains of the palace of Montezuma II, the last emperor of the Aztecs, assasinated by Cortés.*

68 centre *Mexico City. An enormous and touching mural by Diego Rivera on the staircase leading to the upper floors of the Palacio Nacional illustrates the most significant moments in the history of this country, from the magnificent pre-Columbian civilizations to the Revolution and modern Mexico.*

68 bottom *Mexico City. The Basilica de la Nuestra Señora de Guadalupe is consecrated to the Indian Virgin, associated with the cult of the Madonna for more than 400 years. According to the official story in December 1533 the Virgin Mary appeared three times dressed as a native princess. The Basilica is one of the most famous places of pilgrimages in all Latin America, attracting thousands of pilgrims every year. Founded in 1533, rebuilt in 1709 and then seriously damaged by an earthquake, it has been substituted as a place of worship by a gigantic, reinforced concrete structure completed in 1976; it is now a museum.*

68-69 *Mexico City. The north side of the Plaza de Armas is filled by the Catedral Metropolitana, the largest in Mexico; building commenced in 1567 and ended in 1813. It stands where once was the* tzompantli, *the rack used by the Aztecs to display the skulls of the victims sacrificed to the gods. The façade is a rather successful mix of Spanish Renaissance, baroque and neoclassical styles. At the back of the central nave, 360 feet long, is the Capilla des los Reyes, in Churrigueresque style; another seven chapels occupy each of the two aisles. Adjacent to the cathedral is the Sagrario, built in a grand baroque style in the 18th century to house the holy vestments, the cathedral treasure and the bishop's archives.*

70 top left *Mexico City. About twenty miles from the city centre are the floating gardens of Xochimilco, what remains of the lake that used to surround Mexico City. The local attraction, a favourite Sunday outing for many families from the metropolis, are the* chinampas; *these are large rafts covered with earth on which flowers and vegetables are grown as in Aztec times. At weekends a multitude of gaily-coloured boats circulate along the canals, often filled with water lilies.*

70-71 *Mexico City. Grown on the ruins of the ancient Aztec capital, Tenochtitlán, razed to the ground by the Spanish conquerors, Mexico City is the largest metropolis in the world. Born in the absence of urban planning and expanded on land snatched little by little from Lake Texcoco, now practically all dried out, the capital grows every year absorbing numerous small satellite towns into its chaotic urban fabric and climbing the slopes of the high mountains around it.*

70 top right *Mexico City. The Centro Bursatil, the stock exchange, is a building in a futuristic design, a symbol of the ongoing evolution of the Mexican megalopolis; it dominates the city centre on Paseo de la Reforma, one of the main and busiest thoroughfares in the capital, more than 9 miles long and up to 12 lanes wide.*

70 bottom right *Mexico City. The Ciudad Universitaria, situated 11 miles from the centre of the city, has 400,000 students and 30,000 teachers. The University of Mexico City is considered the most prestigious in Latin America and is attended by young people from all parts of the continent. The Biblioteca Central is decorated externally with a mosaic in relief by O'Gorman, and the Rectoría with a mural by Siqueiros.*

The colonial cities, Mexican treasures

72 left *Guadalajara, Jalisco.*
The Cathedral is the focal point of
the city; erected in 1558, it is a mixture
of styles embracing Churrigueresque,
baroque and neoclassical. The two bell
towers, destroyed in an earthquake, were
rebuilt as seen today in 1848. The Gothic
vaulted interior has 11 18th-century
altars, given by King Ferdinand VII of
Spain. In the sacristy is a lovely
"Assumption of the Virgin" (1650)
attributed to the Spanish painter Murillo.

73 *Puebla. The church of Santa Maria*
di Tonantzintla, built in the first half
of the 18th century in extremely
pompous baroque style, has amazingly
lavish internal decoration. Every tiny
part of it is covered with gilded stucco-
work, multicoloured ceramics, mirrors
and figures of saints and angels in an
exhultation of subjects taken from
Christian and Indian iconography
alike brought together in incredible
syncretism.

74-75 *Chihuahua. Capital of the state*
of the same name, with more than a
million inhabitants, it is the city of the
short-haired dogs famous all over the
world and of the norteños, *the Mexicans*
of the north whose music, dances and
cuisine have also influenced the North
Americans across the border. In this
metropolis, the old city centre, a mixture
of colonial style and architecture of
French and art nouveau inspiration,
is now besieged by modern skyscrapers.

72 top right *Guadalajara, Jalisco.*
Right behind the Cathedral is Plaza
de la Liberación, a popular meeting
place, as are the other two main
squares in the old city centre. On one
side stands the neoclassical colonnade
of the Teatro Degollado: inaugurated
in 1866 with a triumphant performance
of "Lucia di Lammermoor" by Gaetano
Donizetti it is now the home of the
symphonic orchestra.

72 bottom right *Puebla. Founded*
in 1531 and capital of the State of the
same name, Puebla is a historical
Mexican city, famous for its production
of azulejos, *small multicoloured ceramic*
tiles. An eloquent example of the use
of this material is the façade of the
church of San Francisco Acatepec, built
in 1730, in grand Churrigueresque
style.

The Indians: half myth, half history

76-77 *Chihuahua. The Tarahumara Indians - who actually prefer the ancient name of Rarámuri, the "men who run swiftly" - are the ancient inhabitants of the Sierra Madre Occidental. Famous for their ritual races which often last several days, they number more than 50,000 and are the second largest Indian ethnic group in northern Mexico after the Navajo. Tarahumara women usually wear multicoloured garments and finely embroidered shawls.*

77 bottom *Chihuahua. The Tarahumara have preserved their customs fairly well despite the often difficult clash with the Hispano-Mexican culture. Mysterious and retiring, they have placed the Catholic saints alongside their gods, bound to nature (Raiénari is the Sun god who protects the men, Mechá the Moon god who protects the women) in a complex and secret devotion. Their ancestral rites also involve the use of the* peyote, *a hallucinogenic cactus that produces magical visions.*

77 top left *San Cristóbal de Las Casas, Chiapas. The market held in the centre every morning is the best place to observe the Indians of the various ethnic groups living on the uplands around the city. They come here to sell the produce of their fields and some craftwork, including the attractive fabrics with flower motifs.*

77 top right *San Cristóbal de las Casas, Chiapas. The expert weavers of the Sna Jolobil, a cooperative of 650 women from the Tzotzil and Tzeltal villages near the city, produce splendid cloths using backstrap looms and also sell their wares.*

The train on
the upland

78-79 *Chihuahua. The Chihuahua-Los Mochis railway line connects these two cities via the Sierra Madre Occidental and the famous Barranca del Cobre, the largest and most spectacular canyon on the continent, larger than the Grand Canyon in Colorado. The railway runs for hundreds of miles on the plateau, in the region inhabited by the Tarahumara; it is not unusual in the stations along the way to see small groups of Indian women, shy and silent, busy making baskets and other small objects, weaving particularly tough grasses together. Others make rag dolls or delightful objects in carved wood and sell them to passers-by.*

79 top left *Creel, Chihuahua. As well as Divisadero, Creel is one of the main stops along the most scenic railway line in Mexico. The whole journey on the sky-blue carriages of the* ferrocarril *which from Chihuahua climbs to the Barranca del Cobre, 8,200 feet high, and from here descends like a switchback gone crazy to Los Mochis on the Gulf of California, is a thrilling ride and a window on the customs and habits of the local peoples.*

79 top right *Barranca del Cobre, Chihuahua. Two trains travel this line in the two directions every day: the Expreso de Lujo, which takes approximately twelve hours to cover the distance between the two terminus stations and the Visitatren, slower and subject to delays. Among other things there is an hour's time difference between Los Mochis and Chihuahua.*

79 bottom right *Sierra Tarahumara, Chihuahua. The construction of the railway started in 1898, planned by Albert Kinsey Owen who thought that he could thus connect these lands with Kansas City. Repeatedly modified en route and subject to constant holdups during construction, the line was inaugurated in 1961. There are more than 200 bridges and tunnels along the 400-mile route.*

From the Pacific to the Caribbean, a land of colour

80-81 *Acapulco, Guerrero. A catchy slogan presents Acapulco as "the place where however much there may be, you will never tire of it". Somewhat bombastic, and although times are no longer those when Johnny Weissmüller, Dolores del Rio, Rita Hayworth, Errol Flynn, Ava Gardner and Humphrey Bogart were at home here, this famous resort continues to merit its fame, if only for the splendid bay.*

81 top *Acapulco, Guerrero.* Los clavadistas, *the famous divers who throw themselves into the sea from La Quebrada, perform every day for the tourists: for just a few dollars they dive into the air from a height of more than 130 feet, brushing past the rocky cliff to plunge into the small fjord just thirteen feet wide where the waters of the Ocean await them. Their falling speed reaches 99 miles per hour and their weight is multiplied by ten at the moment of impact.*

81 bottom *Acapulco, Guerrero. The San Diego Fort is one of the few colonial monuments to have survived the modernist fury that has changed the face of this splendid resort formerly used to guard the maritime traffic which in the 17th century linked Acapulco with the Philippines and the coasts of China and south-east Asia.*

82 top *San Cristóbal de Las Casas, Chiapas. Although not the capital of the state (this privilege is held by Tuxtla) this peaceful city founded in 1528 is the most important economic, political and cultural centre in the region. It is still markedly colonial in appearance with one- or two-storey houses painted in bright colours; those in the picture overlook Calle Real de Guadalupe.*

82 bottom *San Cristóbal de Las Casas, Chiapas. The white and unusually linear baroque façade of the church of La Merced, set between two slender bell towers, stands out against the red roofs of the surrounding districts. The sanctuary, the interior of which by contrast is a myriad of statues, gold and silver, is the object of devout pilgrimages, especially on the part of the Indians from the nearby towns.*

83 top *Cuernavaca, Morelos.
Famous for its delightful climate, this
ancient city can also boast the austere
Palacio de Cortés, erected in 1532 by
the Spanish* conquistador. *After having
been subjected to several transformations,
the palace has now been turned into the
Museo de Cuauhnáhuac and exhibits
relics from the most important pre-
Colombian civilizations as well as
records of Mexican history.*

83 bottom *Taxco, Guerrero. Founded
in 1529, the "Silver City" now has more
than 80,000 inhabitants. A pearl
in colonial times, it now lives almost
exclusively on tourism and the art of
its silversmiths. In 1534 the first cargo
of this precious metal left from here for
Spain, spreading its fame all over
the Old Continent and attracting
adventurers of all sorts in search
of fortune.*

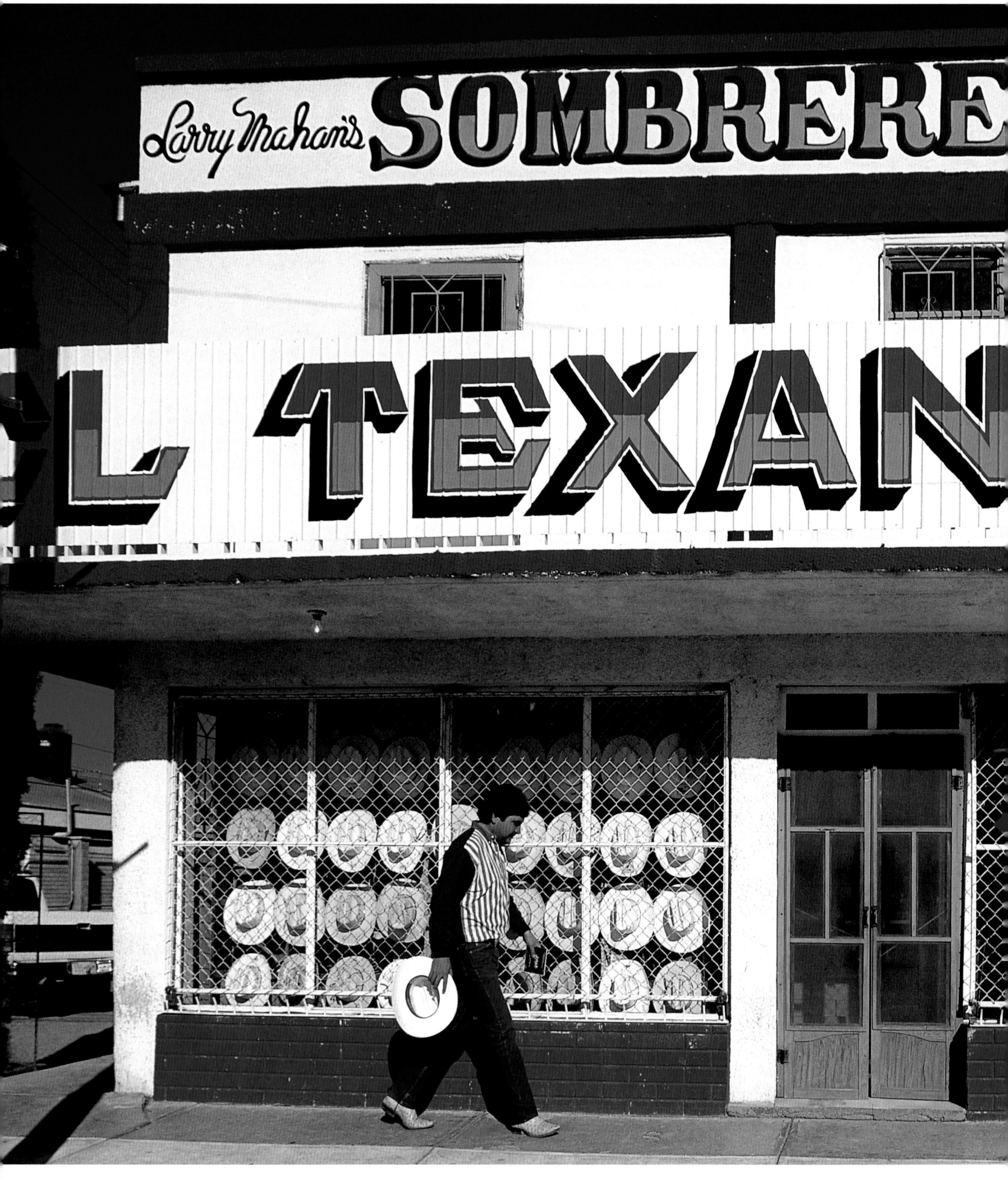
Larry Mahan's SOMBRERE
L TEXAN

Symbols of timeless tradition

84-85 *Los Mochis, Sinaloa. Mexico is an explosion of colour even on the shops and placards. The multicoloured variety of designs and figures that normally adorn façades express a spontaneous creativity and a marked taste for bright colours. It could even be said that the custom of painting buildings in bright colours is as much a part of true Mexican tradition as the sombreros sold in this shop: a tradition that is found unchanged in remote villages and large cities alike.*

85 *Creel, Chihuahua. The products of Mexican craftwork are well known the world over: hats and sombreros (the best are those made with jipijapa fibre in the region of Camino Real, between Campeche and Mérida), dressed leather articles (belts and boots among them), hammocks, trinkets and jewellery in silver, and multicoloured crockery still made to the designs of the pre-Colombian cultures. Whatever the article on sale, the shop must be clearly identifiable and therefore have a conspicuous façade; the bright colours and candid advertising can be considered a popular version of the works of the great contemporary mural artists (Rivera, Orozco, O'Gormon, Siqueiros) whose work represents Mexico's major contribution to 20th-century art.*

Charros, music, dancing and passion

86-87 *Guadalajar, Jalisco.*
In the states of Mexico and Jalisco one can still encounter charros, *the all-Mexican version of the US cowboys. Skilled horsemen and expert lasso throwers, the* charros *wear quality* clothes. *The costumes for the* charreada *are decorated with large belt buckles and with elegant buttons for their boleros and are used to close the trousers at the sides. Floral motifs, sometimes stylized, are highly popular for horse harnesses.*

87 *Guadalajara, Jalisco.*
All the distinguishing marks of the
charros *are of Spanish origin. Sixteen*
horsemen, companions of Cortés,
introduced horses into Mexico.
In colonial times, every Spaniard had
to have a horse, whereas this was severely
forbidden by royal decree for the
Indians. With time, however, they too
became familiar with these animals,
being responsible for their supervision,
and they soon learned to stay in the
saddle and handle a lasso. Just like the
Argentinian gauchos *the* charros *have*
become excellent horsemen.

88 top *Oaxaca. Dancing is fundamental to everyday Mexican life as too is music. The dances, numerous and greatly different from one another, are strictly linked to the different local cultures. The traditional music of the frontier and the* norteño *style have inspired dances with steps that are an extraordinary mixture of polka, waltz, ranch and* paso doble: *a mixture born from the encounter between the Sanish-speaking populations and immigrants from central Europe.*

88 bottom *Oaxaca. More typically native are the dances danced in the State of Oaxaca. The female costumes are gaily coloured, the wide skirts, down to the ground being livened up with tight bodices and low necklines. The men wear all white - the characteristic dress of the* campesino, *consisting of a tunic and tight trousers down to the calf.*

88-89 *Oaxaca. Mexican dances are made of turns and twirls, a display of almost acrobatic ability to the pressing rhythm of the guitars, trumpets and* marimbas. *Often the dances - which become especially numerous during the Carnival festivities organized all over the country - are inspired by stories of clearly Spanish or colonial origin.*

In the name of the conquerors

90-91 *San Cristóbal de las Casas. The heart of the city is Plaza de 31 de Marzo with, on the north side, the Cathedral and its fanciful baroque façade.*

91 top *Oaxaca. The city was founded by the Aztecs in 1486 as a military outpost and later extended by the Spaniards in the customary pattern of perpendicular roads, typical of all the colonial settlements in Mexico. At the heart of the urban fabric are the adjacent squares of Zócalo and Alameda, on which stands the baroque Cathedral; the Alameda in particular from sunset until late into the night becomes the centre of city life and fills with stalls selling balloons, sweetmeats, toys and other knick-knacks.*

91 centre *Tlacochauaya, Oaxaca. A baroque jewel of the 16th century, the church of San Jeronimo has one nave with a barrel vault all decorated with gilded friezes and motifs of clearly Indian inspiration. Altars with multicoloured wooden statues open in the side walls and the transept and precious period paintings have been added between the marble and gilded wood of the main altar.*

91 bottom *Valladolid, Yucatán. This attractive town which appeared in 1534 as the trading centre of the region conserves numerous reminders of its colonial past. Again the Zócalo is the focal point of city life; this large square is dominated by the severe façade of the baroque Cathedral of San Gervasio and its soaring, twin bell towers.*

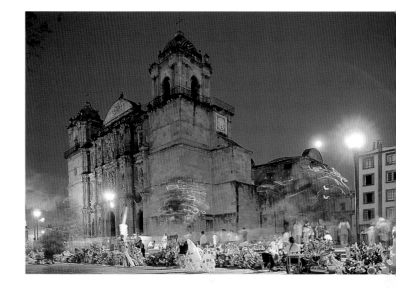

92-93 *Campeche. Drowsy and quiet capital of the state of the same name, laid out along the shallow sea, finally taken from the Mayas by the Spanish in 1540, this city is more than all else known for the oil platforms installed some miles off the coast and for its past bound to the battles with pirates. The ramparts of the old Fuerte de San Miguel in particular still recall the legendary names of grim characters such as John Hawkins, Pato de Palo, John Drake and Captain Morgan, buccaneers attracted by the gold and silver that was loaded in the port of Campeche to be sent to Spain. Their bold adventures are still told in a show of son et lumière held every evening after sunset on the* baluartes.

93 top *Campeche. The seven 18th-century ramparts that make up the fort of San Miguel still stand majestic. The most monumental is the Baluarte San Carlos; inside one can visit the interesting Sala de las Fortificaciones. In the Baluarte de la Soledad, overlooking Plaza Moch-Cuouh is the Museo de Estelas Maya, displaying Mayan stelae and artefacts from the times of the pirates.*

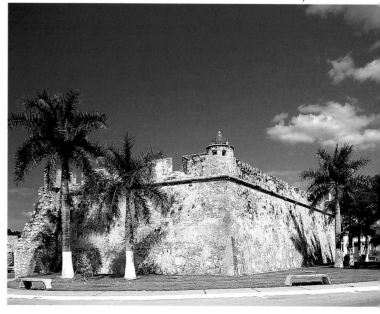

93 centre *Campeche. The din of the pirates' attacks and their furious cannonades still hangs over the massive walls of Baluarte de San Pedro, topped with heavy crenellation along the interior of which runs the guard beat.*

93 bottom. *Campeche. On the north side of the Parque Principal stands the Catedral de la Concepción, with a Spanish tower completed under the Conquerors, and the Campeche tower, completed in the years of Independence.*

94-95 *Mérida, Yucatán. Capital of the state, this heavily populated metropolis is the main market of the region and the starting point for a visit to the ancient Mayan cities of the peninsula. The perpendicular plan of the roads and the style of most of the buildings in the centre reveal its colonial origin. Founded in 1542, Mérida developed as usual around the large square, Plaza Mayor, on which stand the main city buildings and the Cathedral. The Palacio de Gobierno houses an intertesting collection of murals by Fernando Castro Pacheco portraying events and characters from local history.*

95 top *Mérida, Yucatán. The Cathedral was erected in rather severe baroque style between 1561 and 1598 with material retrieved from the Mayan temple which used to stand on this square. Inside it conserves the miraculous statue of Cristo de las Ampollas, the object of fervent devotion.*

95 centre *Mérida, Yucatán. On the north side of Plaza Mayor is the Palacio de Gobierno, the residence of the state governor. Erected in 1892 it has a monumental façade marked by a spacious portico onto which opens a long row of large windows.*

95 bottom *Mérida, Yucatán. Facing the Palacio de Gobierno is the Palacio Municipal, topped by a clock tower. Founded in 1542 and repeatedly destroyed, in its present form it dates from 1850. Every year it is the venue for performances such as the dances of the local folklore ballet and concerts of Yucatecan music.*

96-97 *San Pedro Tapanatepec, Oaxaca. On the Pacific coast, almost on the border with Chiapas, there is a vast salt lagoon known as the Mar Muerto; here in this enchanted corner of practically uncontaminated nature, land blends with the sea and man lives in symbiosis with an ecosystem of great naturalistic interest.*

Mexico in celebration

98 top *In Mexico there are many traditional celebrations (more than 6,000 have been counted!) absolutely all animated by processions in costume, dancing and fireworks.*

98 bottom *Mitla, Oaxaca. To commemorate the Day of the Dead, masked characters let themselves go in the fascinating "Danza de los Muertos" while the public watches the processions advance towards the cemeteries.*

99 top *Papantla, Veracruz. The famous Voladores of Papantla are descendents of the Totonac tribe; on the days of Corpus Domini and San Francisco they tie themselves to a rope fixed and wound around the top of a pole up to 80 feet high and then launch themselves backwards into the air. This produces a spectacular aerial dance, each "flyer" making thirteen ever bigger and faster circles as the rope unwinds. This form of acrobatics has ancient origins and before the advent of Christianity was celebrated to honour the gods, although today it is frequently repeated exclusively for the benefit of the tourists.*

99 bottom *Zinancantan, Chiapas. The* Capitanes *are the principal characters in the solemn religious festival of San Sebastián, held in this remote village on the mountains a few miles from San Cristóbal de las Casas.*

100 top *Taxco, Guerrero. On the Thursday and Friday of Holy Week there are processions of hooded penitents carrying heavy bundles of wood on their shoulders. The religious march winds through the streets of the town from the Church of Santa Prisca and it is not unusual to see many devotees carrying a cross and flagellating themselves: often in Mexico religious fanatism reaches rather bloody extremes.*

100 bottom *Cuetzalán, Puebla. On 4 October, impressive demonstrations are organized here for the festival of San Francisco de Assisi combined with the* Feria del Café y del Huipil. *One of the dances is the* Quetzales, *the dancers wearing large round head-dresses made of feathers, ribbons and reeds. The Nahua women braid their hair with strips of embroidered fabric called* maxahual, *raising their hair until it looks like a hat.*

100-101 *Oaxaca. The numerous festivals celebrated in the city throughout the year are authentic expressions of the folklore and culture of the peoples in this region. One of the most important dates to remember is the feast of the Virgen del Carmen, held in the second week in July with dancing, torchlight processions and fireworks. The two Mondays after 16 July see the explosion of the great festival of Los Lunes del Cerro, one of the most famous folklore festivals in all Mexico. On these occasions the crowd, the splendidly dressed women in particular, offers an extraordinary spectacle.*

102 and 103   *Mexico City. An all-Indian festival dating from the early days of colonization, the celebration of the Virgen de Guadalupe is held every 12 December. According to legend, in 1531 the Virgin appeared to the Indian Juan Diego in the woods on Cerro del Tepeyac, where there once stood an Aztec temple dedicated to the goddess Tonantzin, the mother of the gods, and asked him to build a chapel in her honour. The bishop Fray Juan de Zumárraga would not believe Juan Diego, so the Madonna appeared a second time emblazoning her image on the Indian's white cloak and telling him to gather the roses growing there and take them together with the cloak to the priest. The miracle was acknowledged and since then Our Lady of Guadalupe has been the patron saint of Mexico. The work of converting the indigenous peoples was facilitated by this prodigy and today the cloak hangs over the marble altar in the new basilica, surrounded by tons of offerings in gold and silver. Besides the usual pilgrimages and religious functions on this occasion there is a parade of people wearing the costumes of the ancient Aztecs, in a mixture of multicoloured feathers, breastpieces, leg-coverings and head-dresses; it is their way of celebrating the evangelization of Mexico but also of remembering the ancient splendours and regaining a personal cultural identity.*

Uncontaminated nature

104 top *Cancún, Quintana Roo. The bluest blue that softens into turquoise: these are the colours of the sea that surrounds the tourists' Mexican seaside mecca. Once past the white waves you dive into depths filled with brightly coloured fish and corals, but keep an eye out for sharks!*

104 bottom *Viesca Desert, Coahuila. From the border with the United States to the range that divides the country into two distinct areas, Northern Mexico appears as a vast plateau enclosed between the Sierra Madre Oriental and the Sierra Madre Occidental - a harsh, often desolate territory where rainfall is rare. The Viesca desert is surrounded by low mountains that disappear on the horizon and is particularly arid. Yet, until the last century it was inhabited by the Irritiles Indians whose first archaeological traces date from 1000 years B.C.*

105 *Sateyo, Chihuahua. On the uplands and in the valleys of the north, cacti are the predominant form of vegetable life. In this arid habitat there are more than 101 varieties, of which 60 are endemic: from the Idria Columnaris, which exceeds 65 feet in height to the very small barrel cactus. Cacti grow slowly and can live for centuries, some even reaching a weight of 10 tons and able to contain more than 650 gallons of water, snatched from the ground with their long, ramified roots. They have adapted admirably to the environment: the leaves have become pointed prickles, reducing the external surface to a minimum in order to withstand the high temperatures and transferring photosynthesis to the stem. Some tiny ones have taken refuge beneath the sand and the upper part looks dried out but just a few drops of water will make them flourish again.*

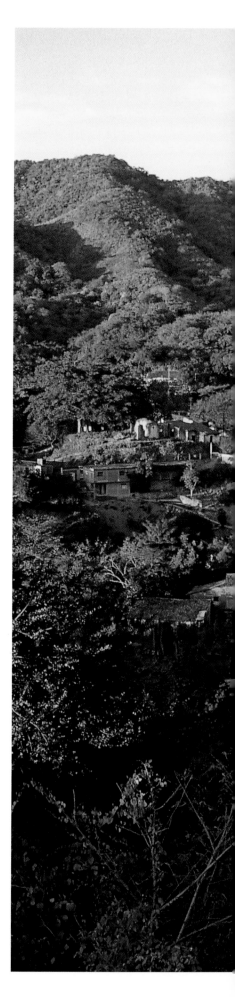

106 top *Barranca del Cobre, Chihuahua. Hawks, buzzards and eagles: these alone command from above this intricate network of valleys dug over thousands of years by the rainwater, rivers and the wind. 1,600 feet deeper than the Grand Canyon in Colorado and four times as large, the Barranca del Cobre is one of the biggest fissures opened in the surface of the earth. For an idea of its dimensions it suffices to think that while on the plateau the climate is continental, at the bottom the temperature and vegetation are typically tropical.*

106 bottom *Zona del Silencio, Coahuila. This is the realm of the puma and the wild mountain cat, golden eagles and the snake of seven paces (so-called because anyone unfortunate enough to be bitten has time to take just a few steps before dying). The only sounds here are the whistling of the wind and the call of the birds. By a mysterious play of the earth's magnetism, in this weird place radio waves are not propagated and compasses and radar go crazy. Bombarded by meteorites that light up the summer nights, the valleys still have millenary fossil forests and drawings by the Mapini Indians dating from 4,000 years ago.*

106-107 *Copala, Sinaloa. Amidst the uneven folds of the Sierra Madre Occidental, on the side sloping down towards the Pacific coast, are some ancient mining towns, almost completely abandoned. After having been exploited, manipulated and harmed, nature is taking back what it possessed, covering man's traces with forest.*

The fabulous sea

108 top left *Huatulco, Oaxaca.*
Small bays, hidden creeks, 100 miles
of unforgettable beaches and turquoise
crystal-clear waters are what this
ancient Zapotec and Mixtec fishing
village on the coast of the Pacific has
to offer. A similar garden of Eden could
not but be extensively exploited and,
indeed, after Acapulco and Cancún,
Huatulco will soon become one of the
leading seaside resorts in Mexico.

108 top right *Puerto Escondido, Oaxaca.*
"Alternative" tourists are attracted here
by the huge waves, never-ending beaches,
curvaceous señoritas *and more ..*
Actually what until just a few years
ago was nothing more than a small
fishing village (it took this name because
it was the only safe landing place
in the region) has now become a crowded,
fashionable seaside resort, but still
pleasant.

108 bottom left *Huatulco, Oaxaca.*
Although building sites are multiplying,
everything here appears to have been
conceived in the name of environmental
protection.
Fonatur, the national fund for the
promotion and development of Mexican
tourism, guarantees that for every area
developed, twice as much land will be set
aside as a natural reserve.
For the moment Huatulco is not yet
choking in the cement and offers relaxing
water sports, including deep-sea fishing.

109 *Huatulco, Oaxaca. Situated in*
a charming position, this resort already
has some excellent international hotels
that provide all comforts.

110-111 *Puerto Angel, Oaxaca.*
Inviting and surrounded by spectacular
scenery, this fishing village has
maintained its fascination intact
despite tourist development. All around
there are only dazzling beaches, small
sheltered bays, unpolluted islands: no
society life, only seemingly enchanted
tranquillity.

The giant
of fire and ice

112-113 *Popocatépetl, Puebla.*
The large volcano rises on the eastern
edge of the Valley of Mexico, 37 miles
south-east of Mexico City.
It has an unmistakable regular cone-
shape, is 17,882 feet high and is still
active; indeed a small, new eruptive
cone formed on the bottom of the
main crater in 1921. Its name in
the Nahuatl tongue means "smoking
mountain".

113 top *Popocatépetl, Puebla.*
The great crater on the summit is
kept free from ice by constant volcanic
activity; although in a state of relative
inactivity, in the past Popocatépetl was
the scene of spectacular eruptions.
Perhaps the most famous was in 1519,
a few days before the arrival of Hernán
Cortés and his army: it is said that the
Aztec emperor Montezuma sent ten
wise men to the top of the angry giant
to read the omens and that only two
returned...
When the Spanish reached Cholula
in October of the same year they were
greatly struck by this mountain
spouting smoke and fire and sent
an expedition to the top to study it.
As soon as the scientific interest had
passed, Cortés, being a practical man,
decided to make use of it and sent more
men to collect the sulphur to make
gunpowder.

113 bottom *Popocatépetl, Puebla.*
The top of the volcano is perpetually
covered with glaciers that make an
ascent quite demanding, also hindered
by the rarefied air at such an altitude.
Rope parties usually start from
Tlamacas, at a height of 1,295 feet,
and follow the so-called Las Cruces
route, a march of at least eight hours
through the most spectacular scenery.

Baja California, a different planet

114 top *Baja California. The undisputed protagonist here is nature: aggressive, wild and implacable. Baja California (meaning lower California to distinguish it from the "upper" one, in the United States) is a narrow peninsula between the Pacific Ocean and the Mar de Cortés (the Gulf of California), 744 miles long and 56 wide, but with fewer than two million inhabitants. Its backbone is an immense cordillera of which the highest peak is Picacho del Diablo (10,151 feet) in the Sierra San Pedro Mártir. Essentially an arid land, with stretches of desert true and proper, it is home to a fauna rich in rare species and flora that consists mainly in an endless variety of cactus.*

114 centre *Baja California. Every year between January and March the grey whales arrive in their thousands in the waters of the Mar de Cortés after an exhausting 5,000 mile journey. These are the largest mammals on earth weighing 30 tons and slate-grey in colour. They come from the freezing Bering Sea to perform their love dances and the females then return the following year to give birth and feed their young. Born after a 13-month pregnancy, they grow very quickly and when the school swims out into the open sea in March or April they are ready to face the long trip north that will end in June. Ojo de Liebre, a water labyrinth in front of the Guerrero Negro salt works and Puerto San Carlos, on Bahía Magdalena, are the strategic points from which to admire the wonderful spectacle of the whales in love. Whalewatchers flock in large numbers, modern Captain Ahabs who have given up their harpoons for powerful binoculars. In 1937 the Mexican government declared the whales a protected species and forbade their hunting.*

114 bottom *Baja California. The Mar de Cortés is scourged with chubascos, tropical hurricanes that make navigation unsafe. The boats of the conquerors suffered when they ventured this far in search of the pearl oysters, which have now disappeared after a mysterious epidemic in 1940.*

114-115 *Baja California. The Mar de Cortés is inhabited not only by whales and sharks but also by sea-lions and seals that bask on the rocks; pelicans, frigate-birds and seagulls fly in the sky.*

116-117 *Baja California. Although narrower, Baja California is twice as long as Florida. The peninsula started to separate from the rest of the continent millions of years ago and this movement still continues, often accompanied by telluric motion. At that time, the tip, where Cabo San Lucas is today, was situated between Mazatlán and Puerta Vallarta; then the movements of the San Andreas fault created the Gulf of California (or Mar de Cortés) into which flowed the Pacific Ocean. As the gulf narrows to the north the tides become stronger and less predictable and the wind is sometimes incredibly violent.*

117 *Baja California. Of the total perimeter of the peninsula only five per cent borders, to the north, the United States; to the north-east another four per cent unites it via a narrow umbilical cord to Mexico. The rest, more than ninety per cent, is surrounded by sea. An incredible, crystal-clear, cobalt-blue sea that has given the steep coasts remarkable shapes, broken here and there by beaches that are for the most part deserted.*

Paradise on earth

118-119 *Agua Azul, Chiapas.*
These spectacular waterfalls created by
the Río Tulija 9 miles south of Ocosingo
are a succession of thundering leaps in
the middle of the forest, where the roaring
waters mix with the screams of monkeys
and the calls of the birds.
The unusual colour of the water is due to
the copper oxide present in the underlying
rocks.

119 top *Río Usumacinta, Chiapas.*
This great waterway that crosses the
region and marks the boundary with
Guatemala is an emerald-green maze on
the banks of which stand many practically
unexplored Maya towns. Tenosique,
a village on the left bank, 25 miles east
of Palenque, is the last outpost of
civilization before the virgin forest begins.

119 bottom *Cañon del Sumidero,*
Chiapas. One of the greatest natural
spectacles in Mexico, this enormous fissure
that opens near the city of Tuxtla
Gutiérrez boasts similar dimensions to
that of the Barranca del Cobre. At some
points the walls plunge for more than
3,000 feet to the Río Grande de Chiapas,
which ends in the hydroelectric basin of
Chicoasén. From above the canyon looks
like an emerald set in the jungle.

120 and 121 *Misol-Ha, Chiapas.*
This splendid waterfall is roughly 19
miles from Palenque, in the Misol-Ha
nature park. Here in the lush, green
jungle the river drops more than 100
feet into a small pool, perfect for
swimming. Amidst the sparkling spray
of the waterfall fly large butterflies with
gaily-coloured wings and parrots with
incredibly bright green feathers.

122-123 *Toniná, Chiapas. A Mayan*
town of the classical period, contemporary
of nearby Palenque, Toniná appeared
in or around A.D. 500 and reached its
peak of splendour towards the end of the
9th century. The excavation works
continue despite difficulties and
frequent interruptions and have
already brought to light two temples of
considerable size, built on the side of a
hill, a ball court and some tombs.

124-125 *Cancún, Quintana Roo.*
This paradise of wealthy tourism was invented by the Mexican government and profiteers in the late Seventies. In just a few years, the 12 miles of white sand on the edge of the splendid Laguna de Nichupté were transformed into a jungle of hotels and skyscrapers of the most bizarre shapes and sizes, dotted with swimming pools and white beaches, tennis courts and golfing greens - the new Acapulco. Cancún, not by chance the same distance from the airports of Miami and Houston, is also known as *the "gringos' paradise" because most of the tourists are from the US. In actual fact, there are two Cancúns, but the first is practically unknown to most people: at Ciudad Cancún live those who work in the nearby "Zona Hotelera", known as Isla Cancún.*

125 *Cancún, Quintana Roo.*
The strip of sand on which the Zona
Hotelera has developed, overlooking
the Caribbean Sea and linked to the
mainland by two bridges, is a luxury
tourist resort par excellence. Kissed
by the sun, blessed with a delightfully
mild climate and close to the major
archaeological sites in Yucatán,
Cancún offers not just fabulous
beaches and a wonderful sea, but
every possible kind of comfort and
amusement that can be bought with
dollars, from night clubs to discoteques
and exclusive restaurants.

126-127 *Cancún, Quintana Roo.*
However incredible it may seem, even
in the midst of this artificial paradise
there is room for the past. Just south
of the Hotel Sheraton, on the rocky
spike seen in the picture bottom left,
stand the remains of a Mayan temple,

and the Museo de Antropología y
Historia has been housed in the congress
centre of the Zona Hotelera with relics
that date mostly from the 13th century.

128 *Mexico is a harsh land, often*
difficult to understand in its most
hidden and contrasting aspects; but
in the meantime it is proud of its own
tenacity and great generosity: a little
bit like its landscapes of wild beauty.